TRACTOR

COLORING BOOK FOR KIDS

THIS BOOK BELONGS TO:

_____

_____

COLOR TEST

TRACTOR

TRACTOR

TRACTOR

TRACTOR

TRACTOR

TRACTOR

TRACTOR

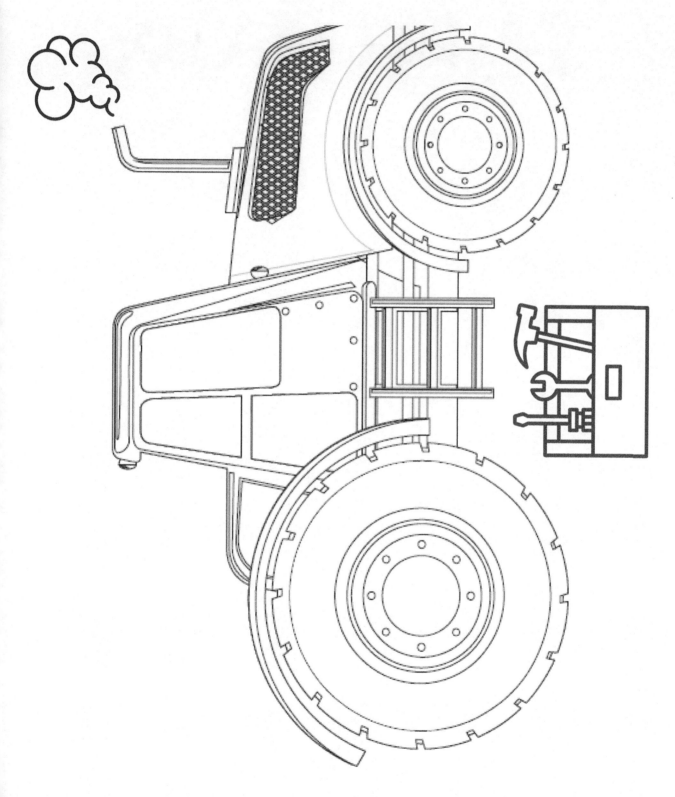

TRACTOR

19

TRACTOR

TRACTOR

TRACTOR

TRACTOR

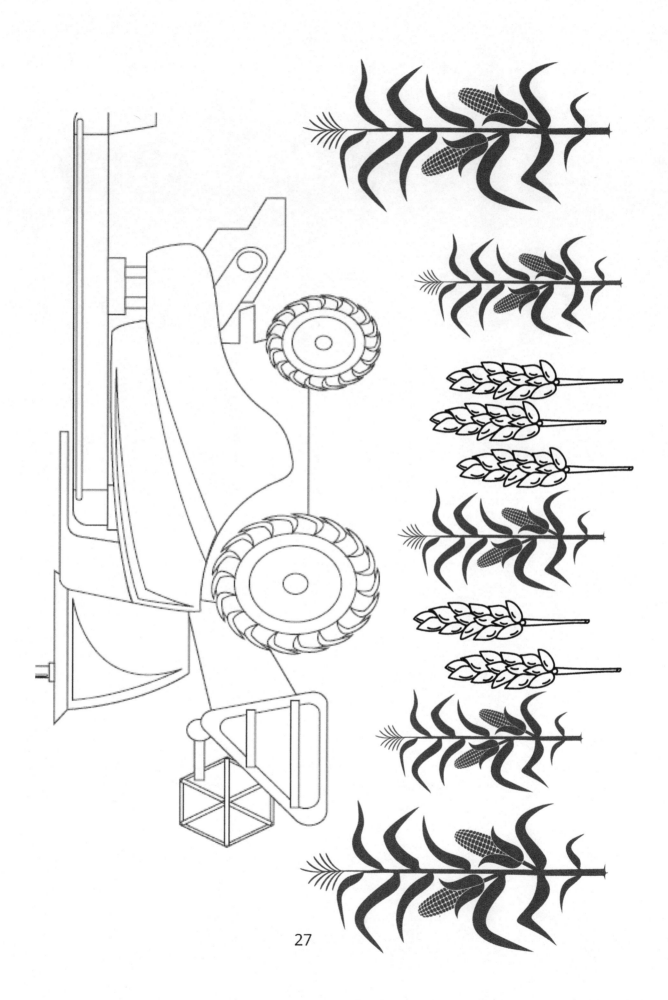

TRACTOR

TRACTOR

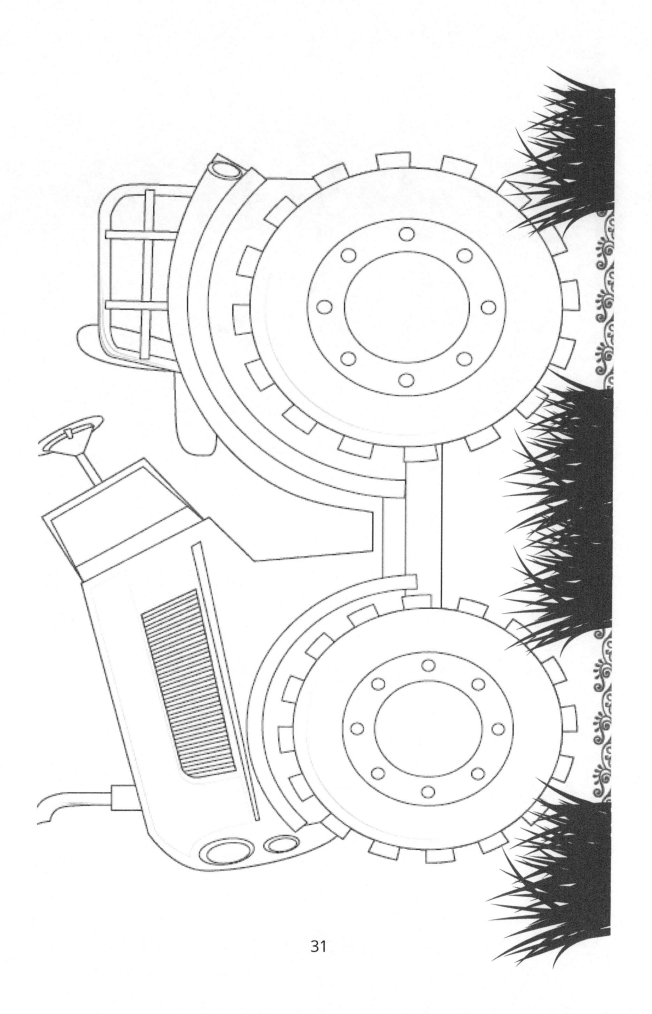

TRACTOR

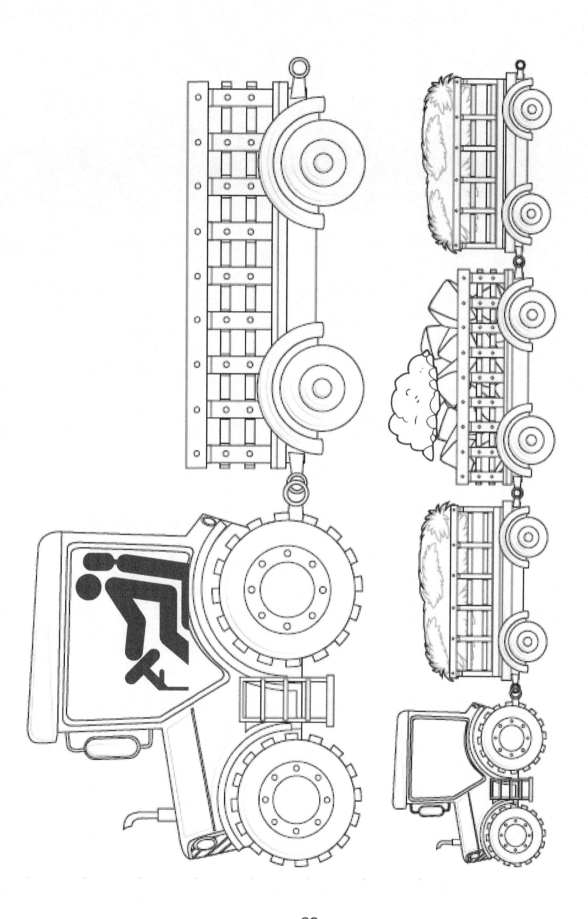

33

TRACTOR

TRACTOR

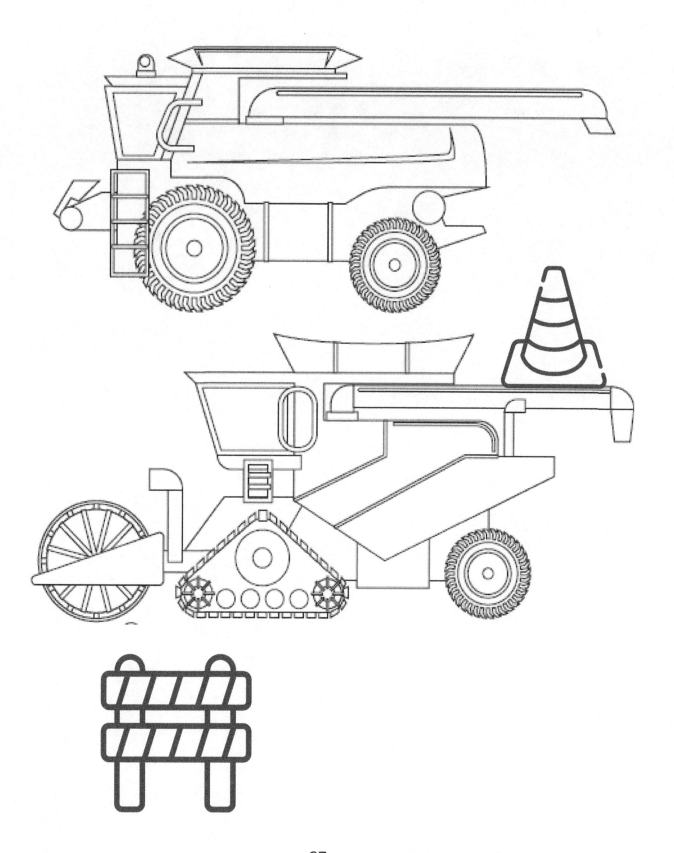

TRACTOR

TRACTOR

TRACTOR

TRACTOR

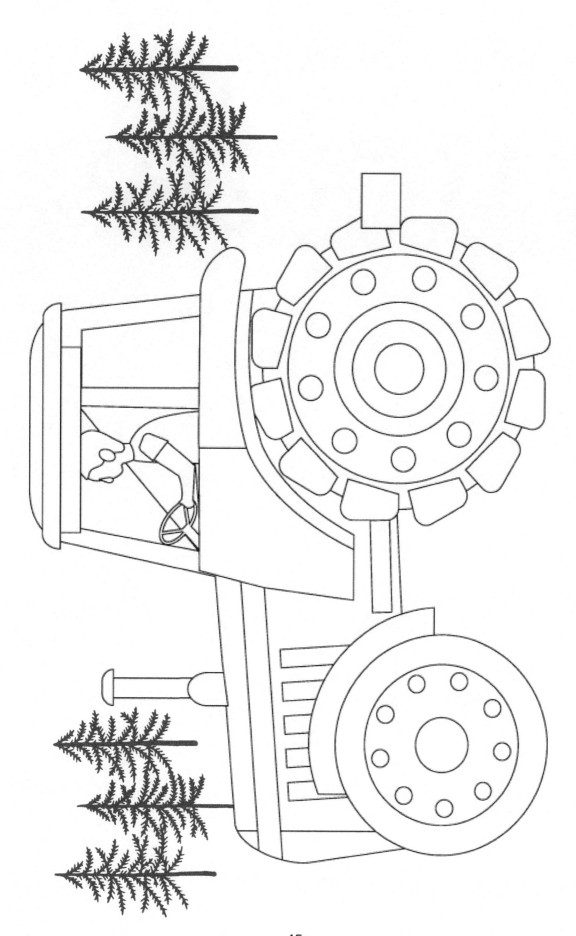

TRACTOR

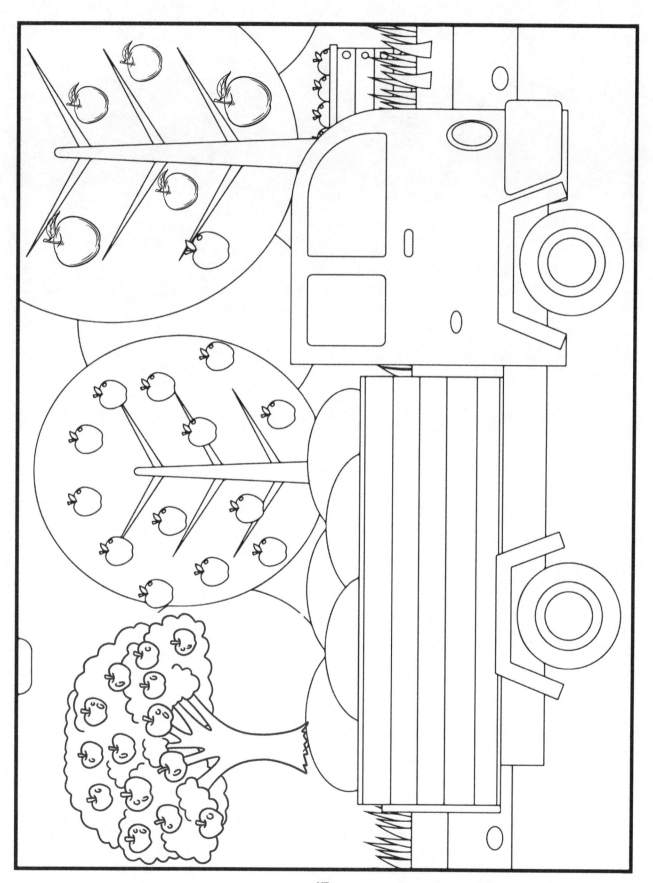

TRACTOR

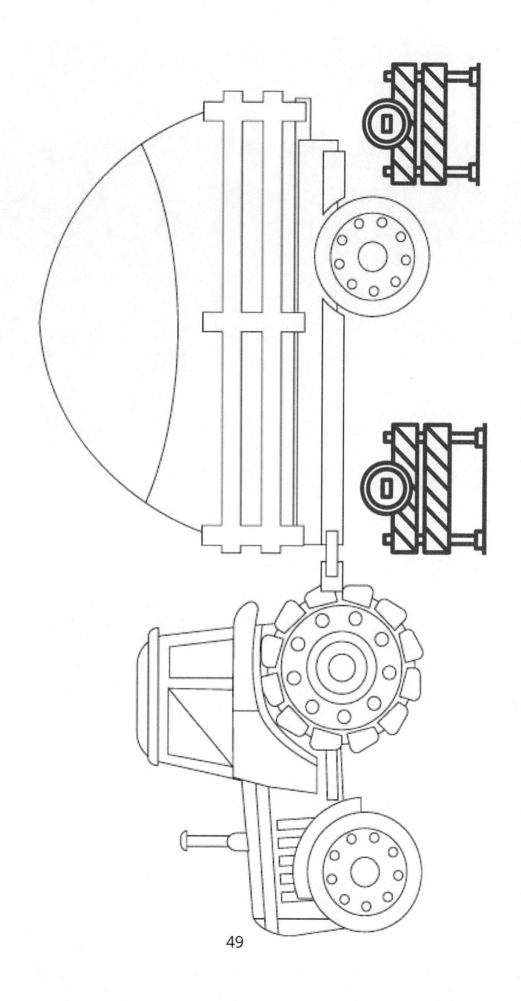

49

TRACTOR

TRACTOR

TRACTOR

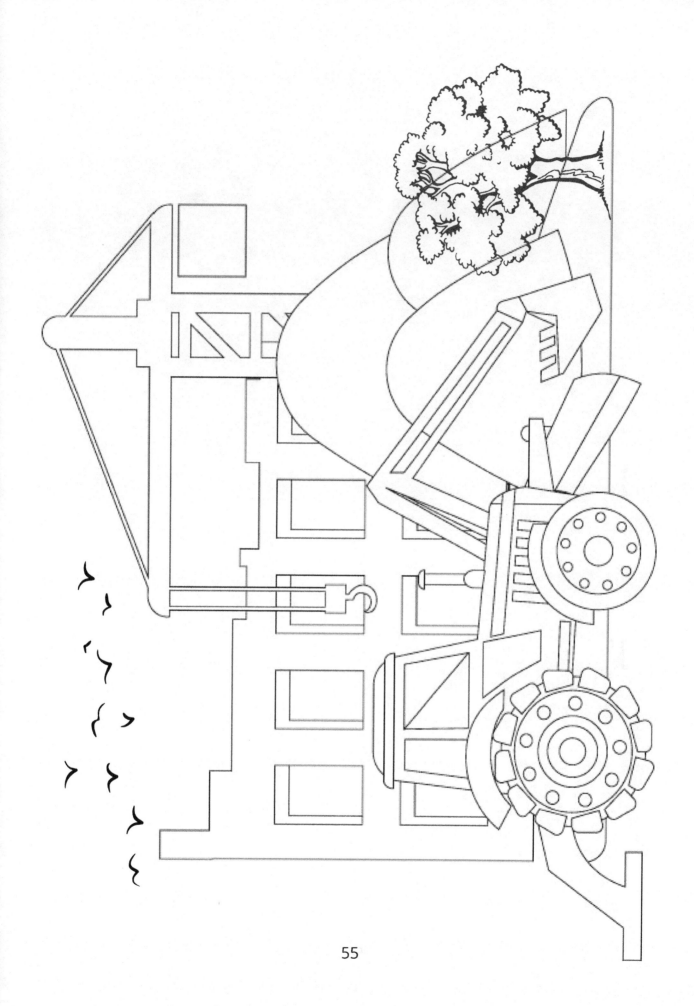

TRACTOR

TRACTOR

TRACTOR

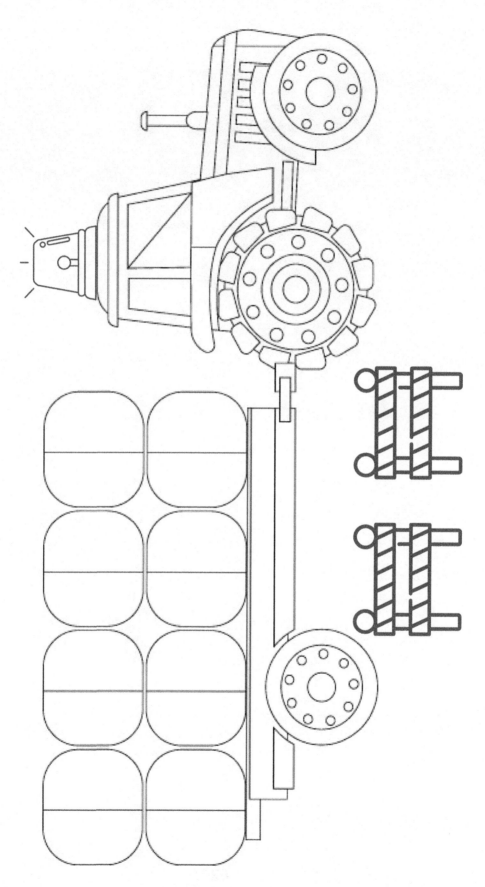

TRACTOR

TRACTOR

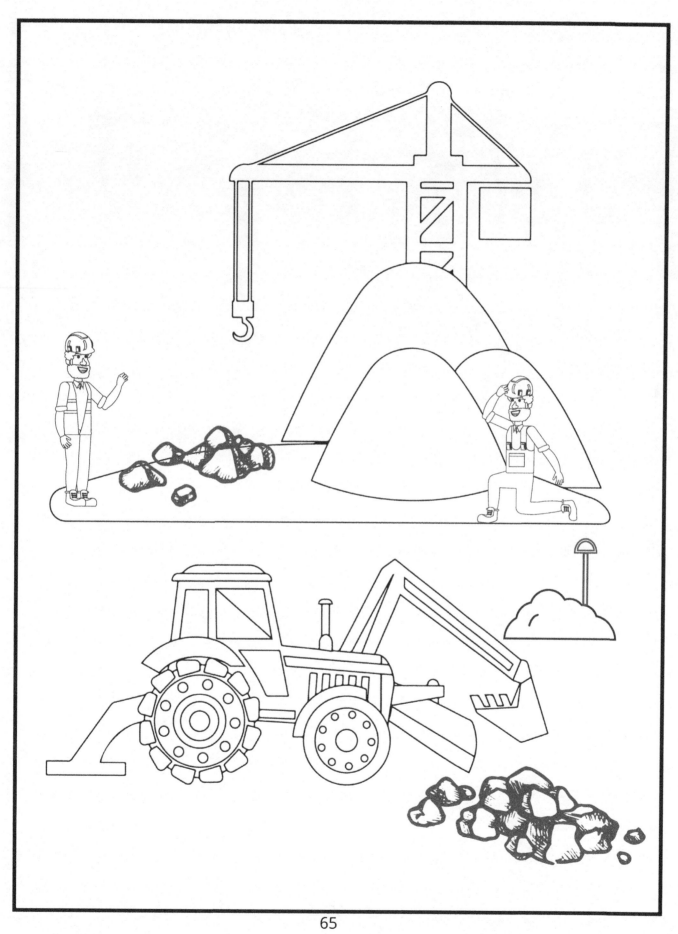

TRACTOR

TRACTOR

TRACTOR

71

TRACTOR

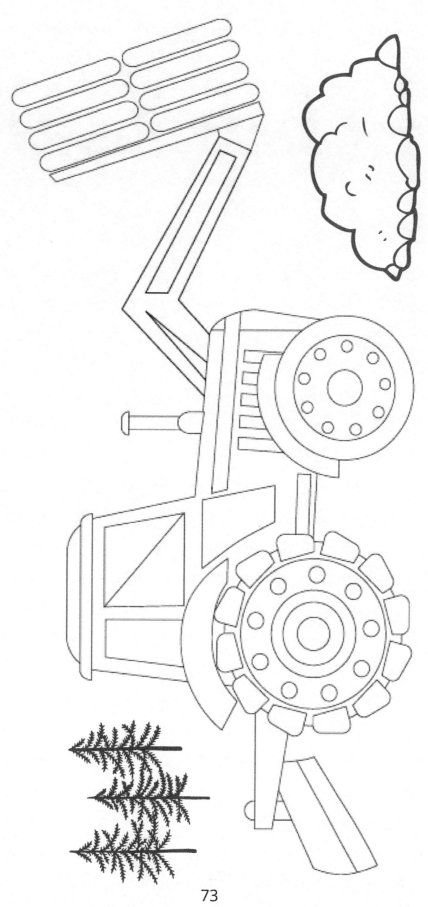

TRACTOR

TRACTOR

TRACTOR

TRACTOR

TRACTOR

TRACTOR

TRACTOR

TRACTOR

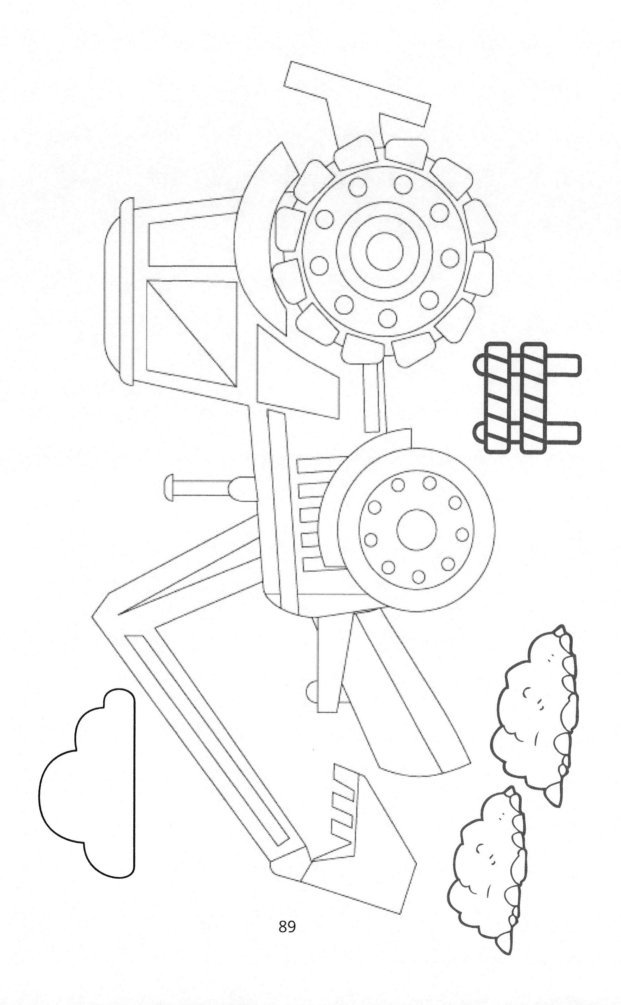

TRACTOR

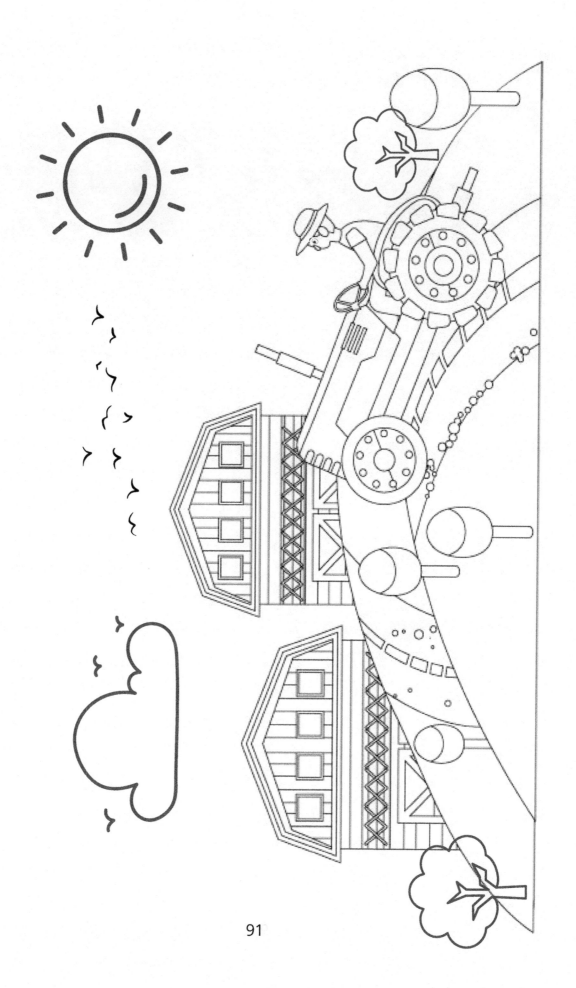

TRACTOR

TRACTOR

Scissor skills

Color, Cut and glue the pieces. Play as you please, there is no wrong or right, be creative!

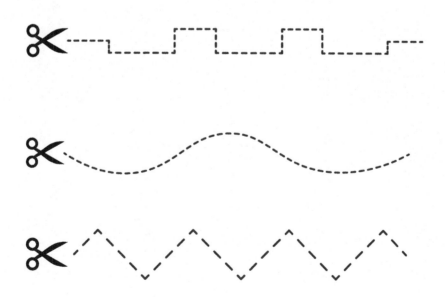

TRACTOR

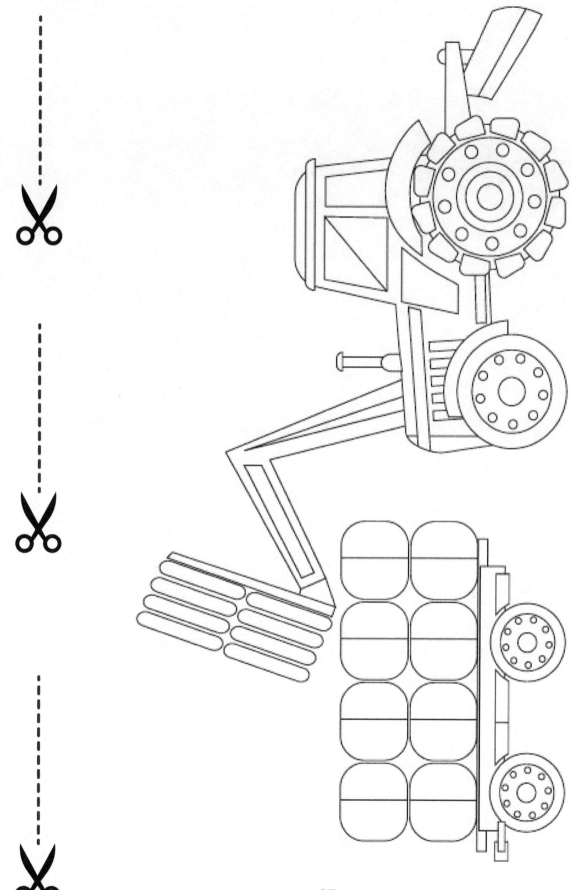

TRACTOR

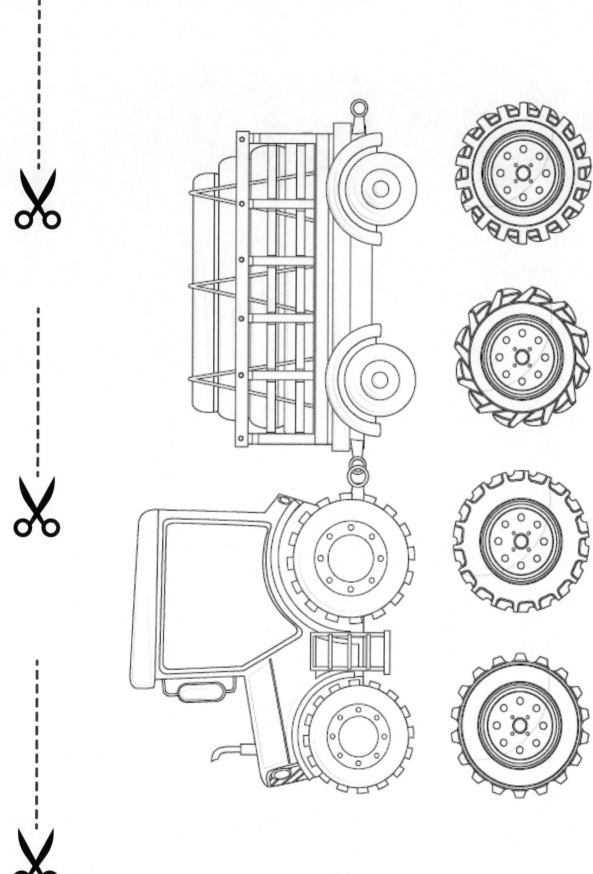

TRACTOR

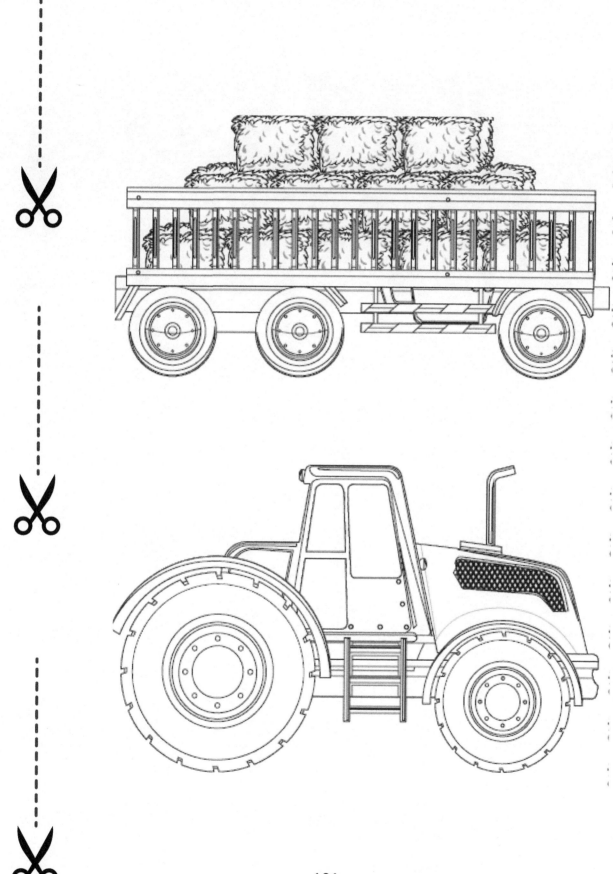

101

TRACTOR

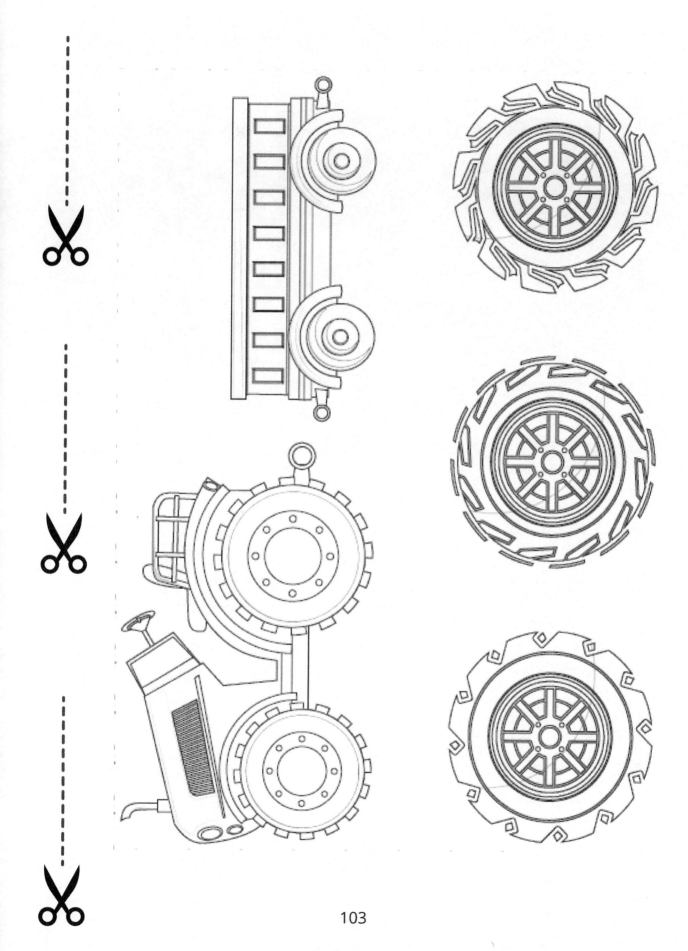

TRACTOR

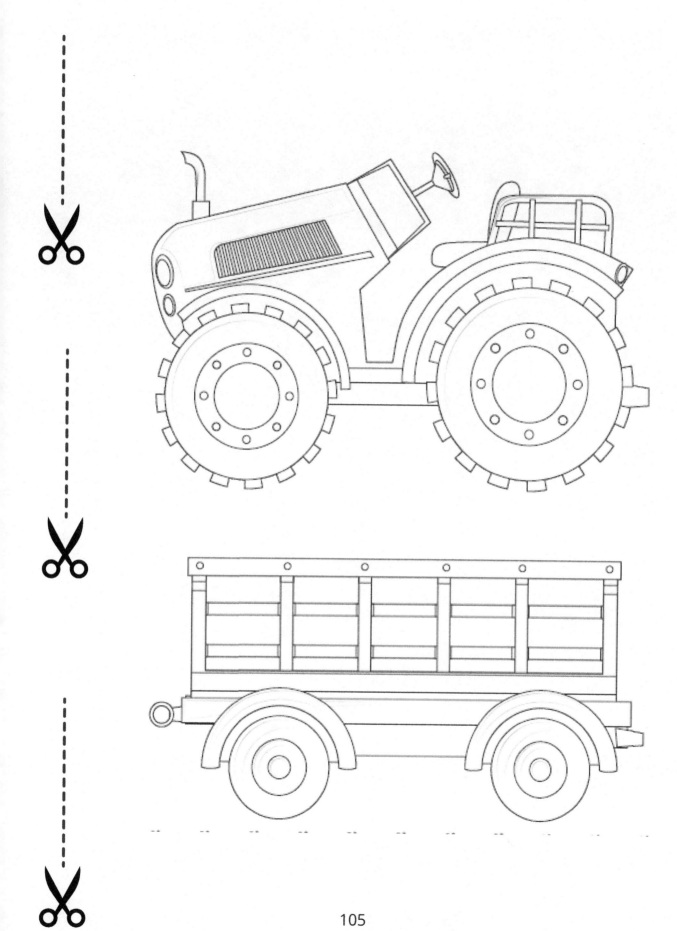

105

TRACTOR

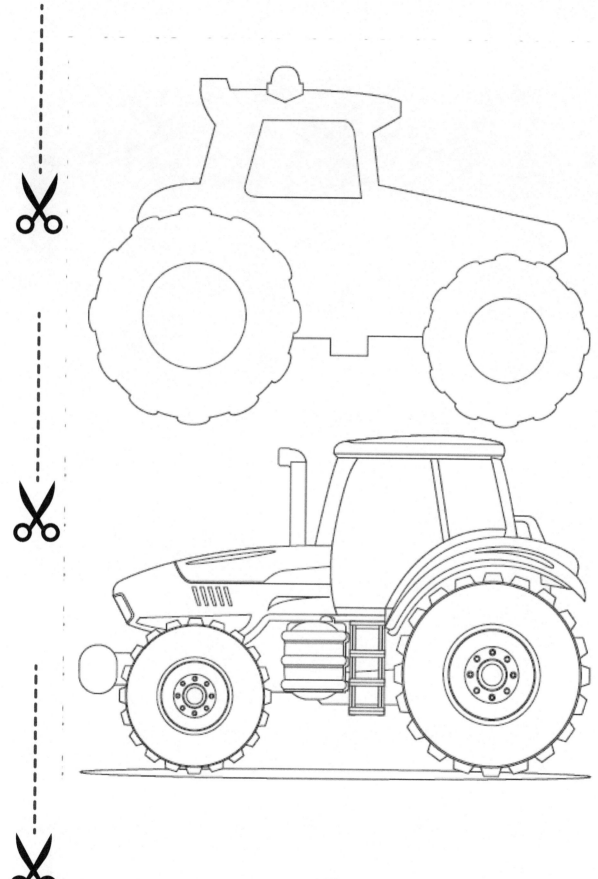

TRACTOR

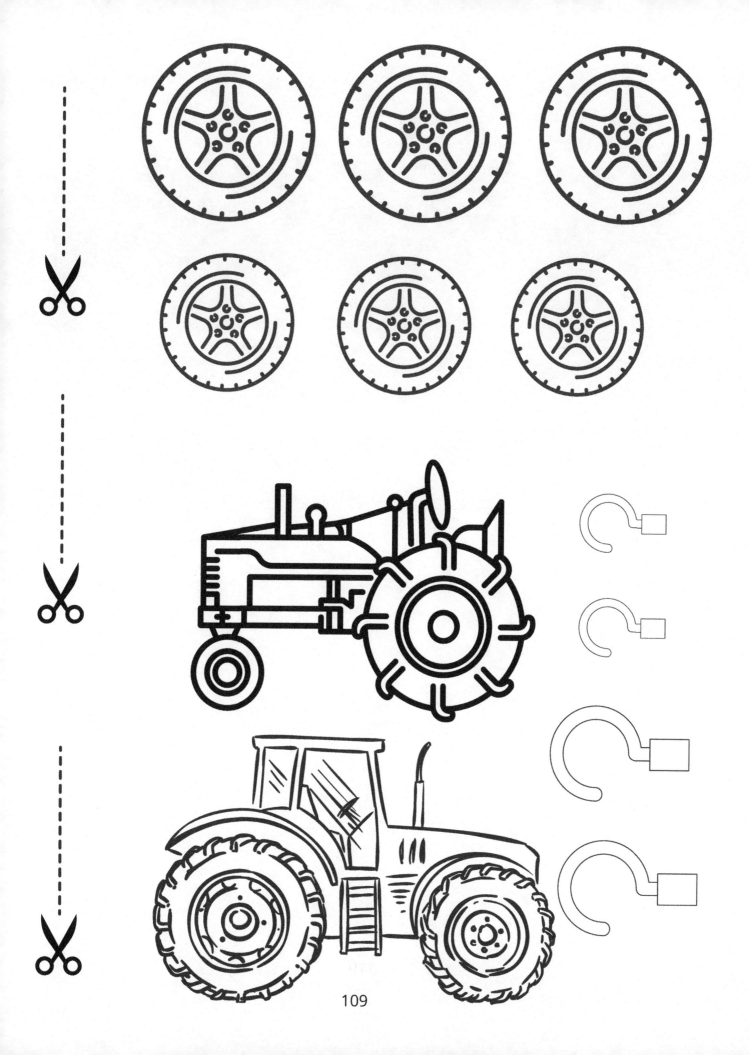

TRACTOR

111

TRACTOR

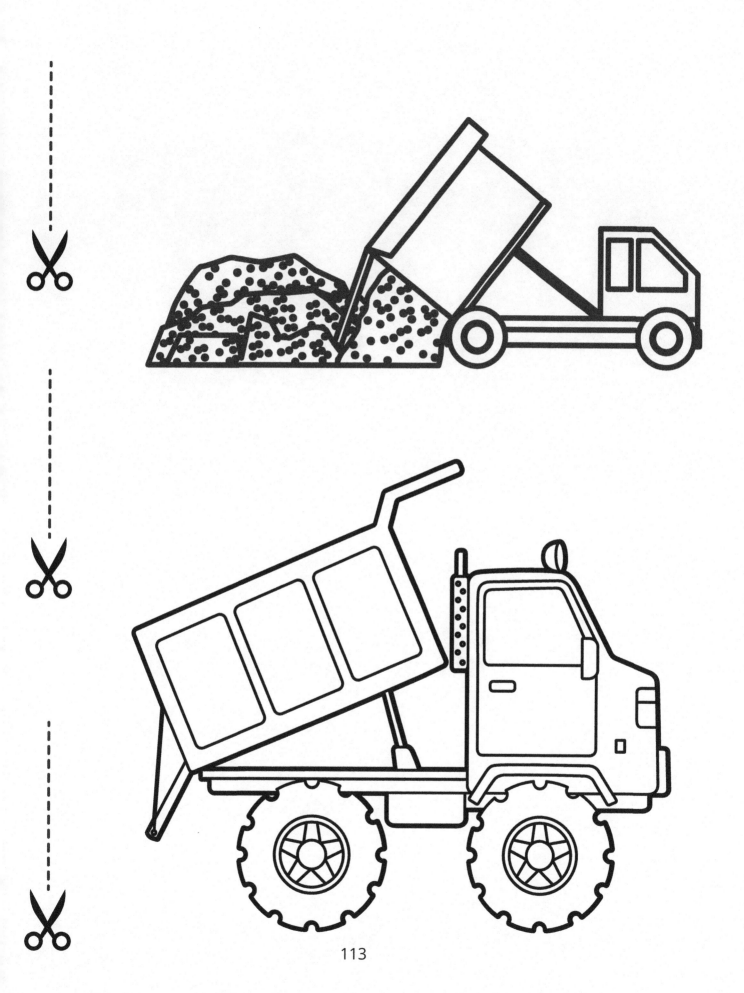

113

TRACTOR

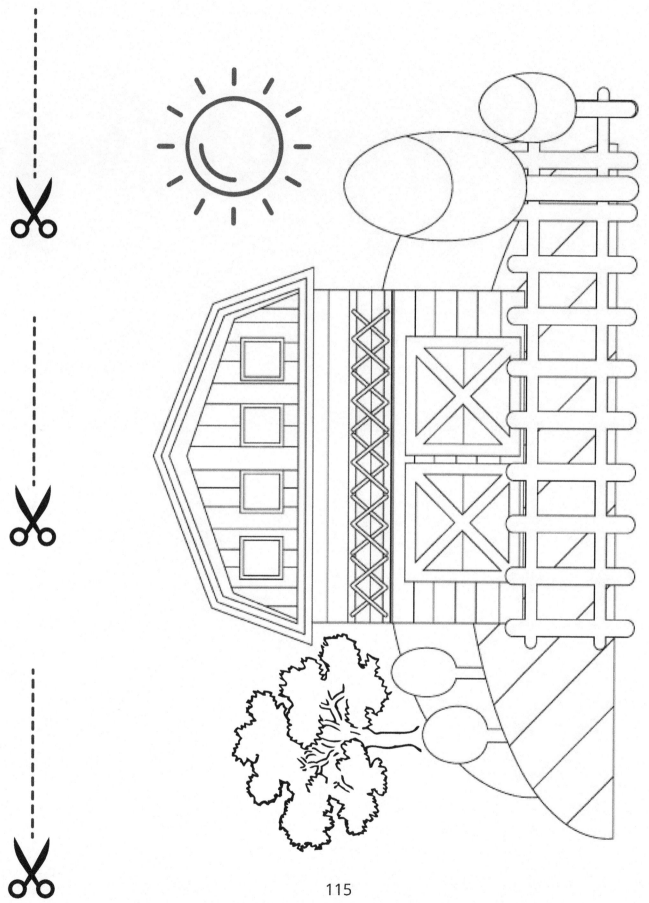

TRACTOR

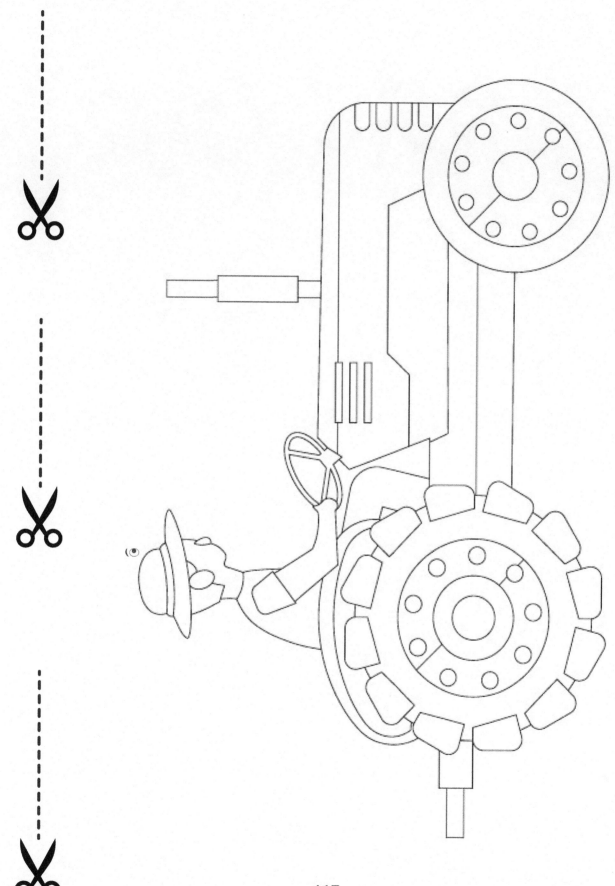

117

TRACTOR

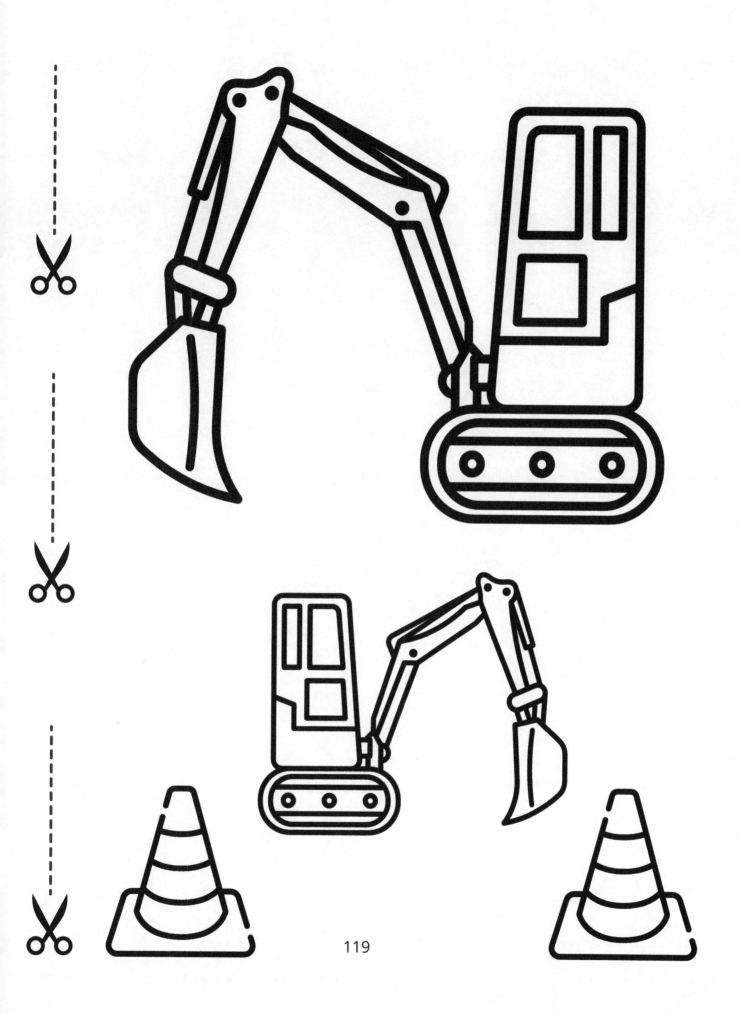

TRACTOR

121

TRACTOR

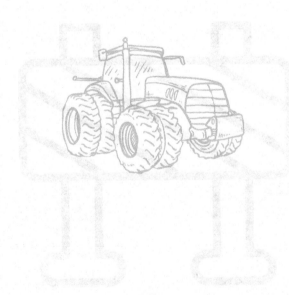

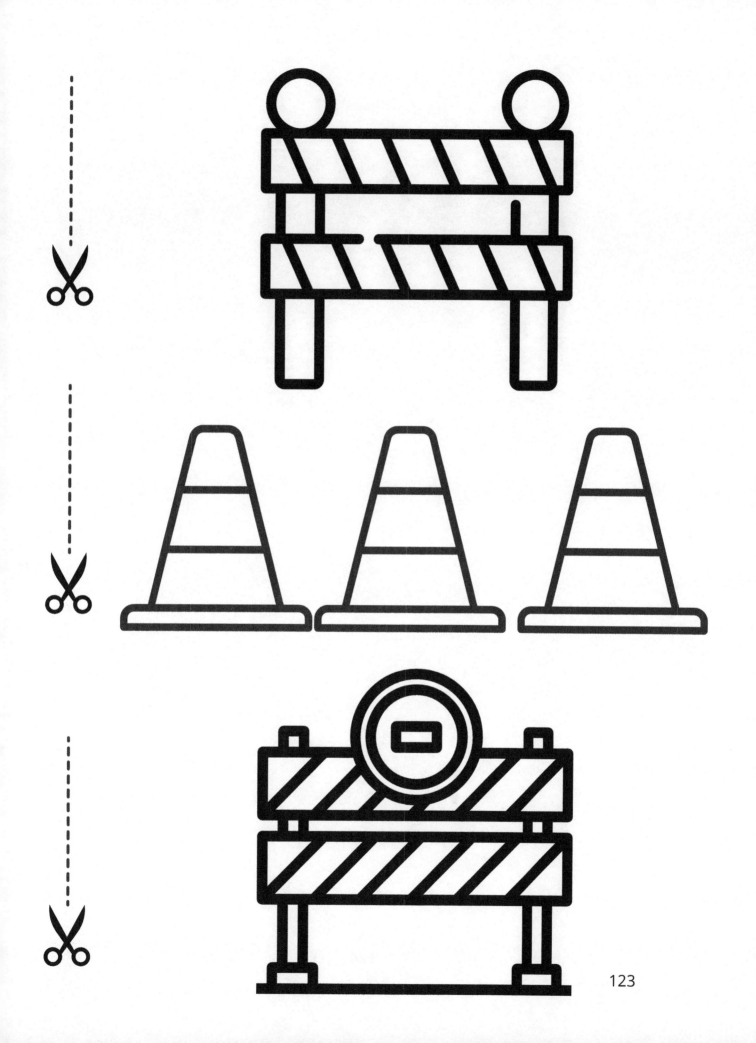

TRACTOR

Made in the USA
Monee, IL
30 November 2023

47820499R00070